Godbless! Garth Hewitt

STEWAR'

`CW00348173`

Stewart Henderson was born in Liverpool in 1952. He has been reading his poetry publicly since the late sixties, and recent tours have included major venues in the UK, the United States and Holland. He also performs on radio and TV.

Stewart Henderson is one of the Directors of Greenbelt, the Christian Arts Festival, where he has also performed every year bar one since its inception in 1974. From 1983 to 1987 he was Editor of *Strait*, Greenbelt's arts and features magazine. Over the past few years he has contributed his poetry to various festivals including Crossfire, Spring Harvest, and The Edinburgh Fringe.

Nigel Forde of BBC Radio 4's *Bookshelf* comments, 'He manages to write without mawkishness about man's relationship with God, he eschews jargon and he tells the truth . . . It's a collection where the best poems are very good indeed, dangerously good; and the worst ones are still great fun'.

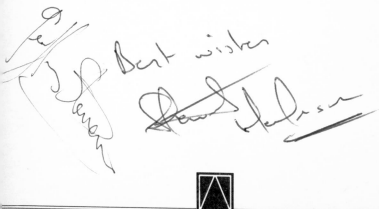

Best wishes

Stewart Henderson

SPIRE

A GIANT'S SCRAPBOOK

SPIRE

Copyright © 1989 by Stewart Henderson

First published in Great Britain 1989

Spire is an imprint of Hodder & Stoughton Publishers

British Library Cataloguing in Publication Data

Henderson, Stewart, *1952–*
A giant's scrapbook.
I. Title
821'.914

ISBN 0-340-50379-3

Printed in Great Britain for Hodder and Stoughton Limited, Mill Road, Dunton Green, Sevenoaks, Kent by Richard Clay Limited, Bungay, Suffolk. Photoset by Rowland Phototypesetting Limited, Bury St Edmunds, Suffolk.

Hodder and Stoughton Editorial Office: 47 Bedford Square, London WC1B 3DP.

Stewart Henderson

A GIANT'S SCRAPBOOK

BY THE SAME AUTHOR

Poetry

Carved Into a Scan
Whose Idea of Fun is a Nightmare?
Fan Male
Assembled in Britain

General

Greenbelt: Since the Beginning
Adrift in the 80s: The Strait Interviews (Editor)

This book is for
Carol and F.M.D.
– lionhearts both –
mother and daughter
who became sisters
and taught me more
about the truth of love
than anyone else

ACKNOWLEDGEMENTS

The following poems first appeared in *Christian News World*:
    'Local Mystery'
    'The Gospel Of Rod'
    'Life As A Snapshot – Those Were The Days'

The following poems were commissioned:
    'Family Matters' (for Scripture Union)
    'If I Should Kiss You' (for the book *In Unexpected Places*)
    'And They Cried For Justice' (for NEAC 3)

Thanks to Rod and Caroline for love, encouragement and inspiration; and beyond words for Chris and Andreas

to Mark and Heather Stephens and Mike Resch for their commitment and support;

to Robert, Jane and Rachel and Charles, whose care, time and Amstrad saved the whole project, and to D for praying.

'Party Night In The Jungle' is for Katey.

CONTENTS

A Giant's Scrapbook

America

Growing Pains

Above The Dove Of Love

A Night's Work

A GIANT'S SCRAPBOOK

GIANT'S MORNING STORY

'This Kingdom sounds all wrong,' grieves Giant,
and so begins another day in his ordinary life.
Giant has had thin sleep,
prodded by a taut night of drumming dreams;
in them life had no land
only spinning seas.
Giant lives in a shapeless city,
one that has been badly shuffled.
He has always lived in cities,
each one louder than the last –
with new darknesses to be better left unentered.
He is used to this one's gnawing noise,
the sliding glass and revving radios of tidy cars.
Giant lives next to a bottle bank.
On lumpy, grumpy, unshaven ground
between a shrivelled church
and a shop that unrattles hoovers,
Giant lies down each emberless evening.
Although quite tall
even for a Giant,
nobody ever notices him;
however, he thinks people are always staring:
'Being this size is a problem,
I feel so large all the time.'
Giant's vision is often faulty,
like that of a short-sighted buzzard
forever swooping on stones
while mice snigger beneath mottled bracken.
'Perhaps there is a city where everything works,'
sighs Giant, expectant of a usual morning being
    pointed at,
'a city where I am the right height.'

3

ON HOLD

Giant does not like telephones
he thinks it's the silences between sentences
that actually communicates.
He says, 'Words are impostors.'
For him the pressing of numbers creates no bond,
only coded forgery,
a numerical illusion of intimacy.
'Telephones are like shouting across barbed wire,'
    muses Giant.
'Frantic information exchanged where no one touches.
We were never meant to be this brief.'
Giant says telephones are in the wrong hands,
'Most things are in the wrong hands.
Judas would have used a telephone well.
A hushed, dusk call from the Garden,
another evening's espionage complete.
Telephones ruin reputations,
get facts wrong
start wars
and, when engaged, devastate the insecure.'
Giant would only give telephones to
shy lovers
the elderly
the lonely
the sick
the cold
and people who plan to die for others.
'And those who conspire on telephones would forfeit
    their sockets.'
Some would say that Giant is simply
not very good at using the telephone,

his big fingers misdialling,
his voice flat with fear,
yet Giant is happy with his observations.

ASSESSING PAIN

Today Giant is feeling under the weather.
Most days, because of his size,
his head is in the clouds.
But this mumbling morning he has a Giant headache.
'Someone has stretched my skin
tighter than a sea-lion's scalp,
pushed slate sharp rocks through both ears
and poured lemon juice into my eyes.
I don't know what's to become of me.'
Giant tends to overstate things,
it's the blood-throb thud of his heart
that's the problem.
It feels too much;
that's where the pain is.

TALKING WHEN THEY ARE NOT THERE

At his father's grave
Giant conducts a one-sided conversation –
   not out loud, but in his head,
the way mourners do.
'When I was young and yelping
you were the truth to me.
Sprawled and bouncing
as a wag, baggy pup was I
under your oiled oak voice.
Your strength kept bears
battened tight in caves.
Compared to you, Goliath had rickets.
When you sat on top of mountains
a new plateau appeared.
However, since becoming a Giant
I don't see you big any more.
Beneath me now your bones are
small white settlements of weariness,
the fatigue that comes from always being in the wrong
   job.
Strange, people don't think of being a Giant as
   vocational.
I've also discovered that tempers
are not obligatory behaviour for Giants.
I was always terrified of yours,
fiercer than sunspots and boiling like molasses.
This has been my inheritance up until now,
to forever roar at slight creatures
in pinafore dresses and squeaking curls.
Tempers are not good for Giants,

they lock the limbs and freeze the spine.
If Giants don't bend, they die.
The gushing goodness of the earth,
too far below to touch.
Is that why you fell?
Starched by anger,
not as a ribbon, but a smitten pylon.'

WHO KNOWS?

Scanning the sour winter sky,
Giant continues his study of seagulls.
He now knows where they go.
Of late he has also taken to counting
the rivets on aeroplanes.
He has also been wondering
where he came from.
Not so much biologically,
but that part he can't touch,
the bit which controls his full reservoir of moods
and doesn't show up on X-rays.

WHEN IT WAS THEN

Giant was once in love.
He does not know if she knew how he felt,
but he thinks she may have liked him
a little bit,
but not all the time.
Sometimes she would be sharp with him.
Then, on the next occasion,
withdrawn,
like a hermit crab who looked out once
and saw only a prowling submarine.
Giant liked it best
when she was soft and affectionate:
he wished this would always be her.
Funny, size did not seem to matter between them,
only feelings:
how he loved her,
how he was nervous of her –
but Giant was nervous of most things.

CORRESPONDENCE

Somebody has written a note to Giant,
it is not signed.
It only says,
'I've known you since the beginning.'
Giant doesn't know what it means,
but it makes him feel
almost content.

REMOTE CONTROL

Outside an electrical goods shop
Giant watches several televisions at once.
On the screens there are
police shooting across traffic,
cars turning over,
sparkling kitchens,
people clapping silently in front of a large golden
    wheel,
houses collapsing,
and a pretty girl trying to be sombre.
They are all looking at Giant.
He hears no sound,
all that moves is what he sees,
and nothing moves him.
Some of it may be important.
But which?
The girl?
The kitchen?
The cars, one now in flames?
Or the people?
Giant goes to the next window
and watches an empty coffee percolator.

NEARLY THERE

Giant's theology is random.
But he thinks he once read
that a bit of God
is a ghost.
'If that is so,' prays Giant,
'then haunt me until I am innocent.'

FIRST STEPS

One day
when the weather was sulking
Giant found a castle.
It was an unusual castle,
much larger than he.
Like a caterpillar to a continent,
there was no comparison.
It was so big
it was as if it didn't exist at all,
so enormous was it to understand.
Giant did not know where it had come from,
but it was there.
'I wonder if it was behind me all the time,
like the moon,' thought Giant,
approaching the drawbridge.
He stared at the vertical wooden planks
for some minutes.
The castle walls had colours not known,
but between the charred, gashed boards
blocked arteries of moss and mildew met.
As he watched
Giant thought he heard singing
like a nightingale's heart being strummed.
The drawbridge slowly began to lower;
it landed at Giant's feet and groaned.
Mournful harmonies now circled Giant
and the ground around him bled.
Giant heard a voice.
It said: 'You can now enter.
This is where you will finally be the
right size.'

And so Giant went into the castle.
He did not diminish,
and as he walked past pillars of flaming glass
a lover's voice spoke his name
and the singing began again.

AMERICA

New York

TEMPORARY IMMIGRANTS

A cab at Newark,
with doors which don't lock properly,
and across into Manhattan's mink embrace.
The streets kick high
with Kern and Bernstein,
and between these silk-scarf poems
Groucho deals gags
faster than a lizard's tongue.
Outside Rod and Caroline's building
a tree has braided itself
with the beauty of the city's fast-tap years.
As imperfect cities go
this is a perfect city,
but where to go for meditation?
The lift, like a dense iron bucket,
draws us up from the swirling well of Downtown,
and we find the harmony we yearn
as we enter the one-floor loft.
Love has happened here
between the bookcases and pillars;
peace, like a cat,
purrs from drawings and chairs;
gentleness is the breath of this place
as the plants surge green,
for when we get too fearful of outside
we will be delivered here.

CITY OF REFUGE

'And New York was the dream that dreamt itself'
(Jerome Charyn)

That was when these buildings were true,
as crammed races gushed through Ellis Island.
Chalk-marked, tagged, kneaded for rickets,
lice-counted, TB-surrounded.
And eventually strained off on to Manhattan's long
    lanes.
In a new refugee camp, without gates,
they threw their cultures up around them
like a womb.
And between the preservation of something fading
and the petitioning of various gods
for protection and prosperity,
into each thrashing cradle was placed
a baseball bat and a subway token,
gifts for an urban christening,
a metropolitan circumcision,
a civic dedication.
On the Lower East Side
Jews wrapped themselves in cast-iron booths,
Little Italy cooked, and fussed about
with scrolls and verandahs,
and along Canal Street clatters of Chinese
shuffled through shops and factories
that couldn't breathe.
These buildings now not cherished for themselves,
but for profit and advertisements.
Yet they stand, feet tapping,
watching the Hudson,

scanning the sky
to see if pogroms or snapping generals
have despatched more of the fleeing and dishevelled
towards their fraught, wrought fire-escapes.

UNDERNEATH IT ALL

The train stops at 42nd
An emaciated man,
possibly in his late thirties,
climbs on with appalling difficulty
He is wearing a dirty cream shirt
and stained, flared mauve pants,
he has no shoes or socks,
and holds a small, styrofoam cup.
The doors close
and he addresses the half-full carriage,
some of us look at each other
Outside the subway darkness
sounds like a continent of rattlesnakes with a
     microphone
'Ladies and gentlemen'
his voice is an undernourished rasp
'I have, as you see, AIDS, and I have no money
for either food or medical attention,
please could you help me?'
He waves his pleading cup at us
like a truce
his soft, brown-eyed face is that
of a haunted labrador
He steps back for care of touching us.
Several get up from their seats
and give him money
A small queue develops
and a final supper without elements takes place.
Someone places a hand on his back,
he smiles,

it is almost no longer a body
but a stooping, silver-hard xylophone
and something in me is unchained.

GRACE CHURCH, MANHATTAN

Last night, during dinner,
a cat lay down off Broadway
From a tree it fell
off its willow wall
to kiss the grave ground
with a parachute full of holes,
the sort of death cartoonists use
for poor jokes.
Now, the soft stains of morning
slide down from the altar window
explaining the nonsense of sepulchres
Outside, a retching siren
swerves past slumped doorways
where the homeless are buried
I look around to make sure
I am not being watched
and put in a request for
the perfect end
one without blood
or mourning.

A WAY OF BEHAVING

New York,
blatant sinner
and fast-talking rabbi,
those who don't die here
begin to anyway

Dylan Thomas,
drunk stiff
in the Chelsea,
emptied out of words,
all cadging complete

Auden,
hungover,
on speed
and between boyfriends,
always
poems and Sunday prayers.

SATURDAY IN SoHo

West Broadway promenades
in the red-plum afternoon sun
Up and out of towners
bring a conviviality,
a colonial civility,
to its gelled and cat-walk sidewalks
The galleries are menus
garnished with the latest abstract dishes
chunks of metal
curved colours
linear shades
white holes
their aloofness beckons people in
On the corner of Spring
Martina Navratilova is being interviewed
Around her a film crew has formed
an engrossed crescent
Everything in her and of her shines
from her thin-as-a-negative black leather trousers
to her blonde, gracile hair –
as transparent as a honey bee's wing –
the sun continues to heap praise on her body
Behind her, out of vision,
there moves a more brittle slightness,
a young, blotch-bearded man
crumbling towards death
slow-marches past on sticks
Slightly ahead, a buddy guides him through
the crashing crowds like a voiceless dolphin.
From then on
I see only this
and it is hallowed.

A LITTLE BOTHERED NEAR
FIFTH AVENUE

I will do anything to attract your attention
pummel a Pharisee
race ostriches
wrestle pompous cathedrals to the ground
pray until I pass out
but don't leave me alone with this man I've created,
this disintegrating disciple.
I will forget theology
and barter if you want
I'll find the creep who made the cross,
then dig up the tactician who said
'Hiroshima and Nagasaki'
I'll sleep with Lazarus and say
'Don't worry. He's on his way.'
But inviolable Christ of the self-inflicted,
please speed me past this tombstone torment
and the eerie reasoning of Hell.
Like a forest fire
I am now too indiscriminate
with my rancorous flames
Let me approach your throne,
blindfolded,
and carve my initials on your footstool,
my name may have slipped from your memory.

PAINTINGS

Metropolitan Museum

In a room of Rembrandts
Liquid light shines from nothing
but brush strokes
a spirit mixed on a palette
illuminates us
From something flat and framed
truth glistens

Wooster Street

Trees' branches weave risen wings
and cup the sapphire sky
lines cross the canvas
and create crowns of water lilies
for whales to wear
colours with no end
from somewhere more than here

Greenwich Street

A radiant heart drips hope
like a joke
over charcoal suburbs
Mickey Mouse's sanctum corrodes
and waits for the right builder
A painted portion of Proverbs
with no words needed

Florida

FEAR OF CLOTHING IN ORLANDO

On the Orange Blossom Trail
the mud-flaps of a titan truck testify
'Jesus carries my load'.
Today the sun is fuming,
fist-shaking, and grinding its gold fillings.
Lunch-time cars sweat and slither
through its molten mood.
Further up the Trail,
outside a windowless strip-joint
that looks like Siamese mobile homes,
a lean girl in scraped stilettoes and thin robe
scurries out of a door
along a stretch of dark purple wall
and in through another door.
She runs almost too fast,
it is not a comic dash
but, like a vole, half mad,
sensing the judgemental swoop of an owl.
It is as if she realises
the consequences of the light
and she has assumed it will not accept her.
On we drive, past a gun supermarket
and 'Hub Cap City'.

LOOKING LEFT IN FLORIDA

The hot-blood, humid night shrink-wraps the body
and the skin's pores go down for the third time.
As I walk through this suburban swamp,
with its remote-control garages
and stanley-knife grass
I imagine being struck by satanic snakes
who rear up like lamp-posts,
or charged by five-geared alligators,
for they are not far away
they are over the road
in the chest-high, scheming scrub.
This morning I saw an armadillo
as you would a fox in Teddington,
it snouted and gulped at the verge,
a contented leather hoover,
a large hedgehog in a crash helmet,
but this is now the cricket-creaking night,
a notoriously bad time for comfort and sweet images.

I cross the dual carriageway
and head for the supermarket
cars are pulled past me,
a chrome and cooled chain
being wound to their separate destinations,
I notice that I am the only walker.

On the way back
I pass a blaring bar,
legs-apart male music is beating the garbled
    customers,

a blurred video screen shouts a smudged green
    astroturf ballgame,
blazing fruit machines call the faithful to their towers
like electronic muezzin.
Between drinks everyone seems to be wailing
and crammed with violence
Earlier in the day
I had spoken to High School students
of poetry and understatement
Now I am disordered.
Vehicles approach me.
In a creeping Buick, Charles Manson, Mark Chapman
    and John Hinckley
are casting lots for the first bite,
screaming rednecks in convertibles cruise past
    demanding,
'Hug a South African secret agent for Jesus . . . or else'
America, if you're free
why are you so intimidating?
I speed my pace
and all thoughts now are terminal.
Lee Harvey Oswald's crumpled catch,
Richard Speck's gaunt gaze,
Son of Sam's handcuffed sneer.
How deep this fearful demon is within me.
I ask my memory to run the Keystone Cops
for respite and laughter,
but it keeps breaking down.

A car actually does stop,
it is matt-grey and pointed,
 a young, long-haired girl gets out
'Hey, wait a minute, can I take you anywhere?' she
    suggests.

Inside me everything vomits,
my crimson wet kidneys turn white
and all around I hear the sick swish of machetes.
I rehearse a line which sounds rational
'I don't want drugs, I don't want sex, and
I don't know Jimmy Swaggart'
Instead I remain silent and attempt to walk on very
   quickly.
The girl persists with her invitation.
'Listen, I recognise you. You were at my school today. I
   just stopped to warn you not to walk around here at
   night. Don't walk most places in America.'
The colour returns to my innards
and I thank the girl for her care.
All inside has now become quieter.
Like me, America is frightened of itself,
and I realise when free of old fiends
I can walk anywhere.
The night still burns,
but it's no longer personal.

NOTHING FANCY

A red admiral*
creeps along a bobbing branch
like a pedantic tightrope walker.
Through the fanning leaves,
a gauze of green,
his careful claws are those of a
crab tapping compressed sand
before the next slow, safe sidle.
He curtails his slow-motion shuffle
and lifts his cherry body to the air,
a small meteor against the sky,
blown glowing by unseen bellows.

*red admiral: bird in Florida

37

DANCING IN THE STREET

A sponsored television programme tells me
that if I subscribe to a course of beauty
home-care treatment I will feel 'lit from
within'. There are shots of a therapy
session in a soft pastel room, where
about twenty women are gathered.
Everyone there made-up is made up.
Some are crying, saying they now

'feel valued, in charge of themselves, precious'

Meanwhile, in the paper, a small notice on
the showbiz page reports that Martha
Reeves is playing in a club in town. Tick-
ets are $5 each. Legends get cheaper.

'feel valued, in charge of themselves, precious'

AN ATHEIST AT EPCOT*

On the seventh day, he rested,
in his kingdom of neat queues
where nobody reads
and all are invited
to enjoy the wandering worship
of his creation
And the nations gather
in his day-ticket millennium
to breathe the incense
of his folksy doctrine
and listen to compact commentaries
about coral, the earth's core
and how to grow root plants in the air
And the people pray in revolving temples
and hum 'What A Wonderful World'
And films are shown that explain
the inextinguishable mysteries of the cosmos
in four minutes
And he saw that it was all very good
and then . . . he pegged out,
only to enter
the celestial theme park of eternity
or, something like that.

*EPCOT: Experimental Prototype Community of Tomorrow, within
the Disney World complex, in Florida.

THERE'S ALWAYS A RADIO ON IN AMERICA

There's always a radio on in America;
the whole country tuned to freeways
that dream for you.
Apart from Tom Waites,
there are few nervous lyrics
seated at roadside restaurants,
besides, it's hard to whistle, wistful hopes
or to dwell on momentary depth
in a room shaped like a donut,
circular
without end,
a formica wall of sugar-death
ridden by revved-up waitresses.
You can be restless or content in America,
never both.
But you can eat.
America does not want to go hungry again.

There's always a radio on in America;
in the seam-straight cities
sex therapists invent new positions for guilt,
for after adultery comes
'the need to diffuse personalised responsibility'.
Out on the righteous plains
the gospel grumbles at those
'Who roll in the honey of sin'
and
'Today's rain activity is a suggested 1.2'

There's always a radio on in America;
one that's never switched off,
polite and optimistic,
even lavatories sing at you.
It helps take your mind off being confused.
Confusion, like conviction, changes people,
all that once was no longer,
ripped down
destroyed
something new
maybe that's why
there's always a radio on in America.

GROWING PAINS

AMO, AMAS, AMAT

Fog river, gown-black stone school
with turrets and lead window bays
A daily dungeon of Latin,
bullying,
and school dinners
prepared from the Hades cook book,
full of stones and brown things,
surely we were all damned
because they made us have seconds.
Opposite, a Catholic grammar
with statues of Mary
bustling boys
through the valley of the shadow of the Crucifix
and into lessons
And as sure as the blood of the martyrs
every 12th of July
fists and feet whirled like vicious windmills
and the occasional brick would bounce
through the mêlée
To the propagandists, it was 'a riot'
the police, 'an incident';
the Liverpool Echo, 'a skirmish'
I called it frightening
but I didn't let on.
Eventually, out would rush
a puffing priest or a Dan Dare prefect
to restore ecumenicalism
And, like all long wars
the point of pointlessness had been passed
and the troops no longer knew
why they were fighting

But the opposition called us
'Billy's murderous heirs'
or was it 'hairs'?

GOING ON THE SUNDAY SCHOOL OUTING

Duffle bag packed and a shilling to spend because I'm
going on the Sunday School Outing
my sandwiches are egg, but I wanted stuffed pork roll
going on the Sunday School Outing
and it's off to the Wirral, that's miles away from here
going on the Sunday School Outing
through the Tunnel we go, on a double-decker bus
going on the Sunday School Outing
and I can sing upstairs though I don't know the words
going on the Sunday School Outing
tunes like The Quartermaster's Stores, and Ten Green
    Bottles
going on the Sunday School Outing
we'll see the river Dee, and then have our mini-rolls
going on the Sunday School Outing
we'll race and fight like pack dogs, whilst the girls play
    rounders
going on the Sunday School Outing
we know no dirty jokes, but we will in twelve months'
    time
going on the Sunday School Outing
who needs religion, when I'm as happy as this through
going on the Sunday School Outing?
it's half past eight at night, as we ride through
    Bebington
coming from the Sunday School Outing
and the sun's crash-landed just behind Birkenhead
returning from the Sunday School Outing
my arms are all sunburnt, but I've still got the shilling

coming from the Sunday School Outing
that means tomorrow I can buy a Superman comic
I've been on the Sunday School Outing
and I'll relive it all as I try to stay awake
after the Sunday School Outing
I lost my mug on the Sunday School Outing
and my mac on the Sunday School Outing:
I can't wait for the Sunday School Outing

WHEN IAN ST JOHN WAVED AT ME

From my muffled, balaclava bowl,
as wellingtons seemed to scrape down to my soul,
a polar bear, ice day turned as warm as a bee
when Ian St John waved at me.

Along Annie Road before the game
limped the Hampden Halo with the sacred name,
but he span round like a deer, though injured you see,
and Ian St John waved at me.

Some weeks later he's back in the team,
I become the owner of a schoolboy dream
via the badge from his shirt I embroidered 4B
with tales of The Saint and his chum, me.

'I've been to 'is 'ouse.' 'Liar.' 'I'm not,
I've seen 'is trophies . . . 'e's norarfgorralot,
and next week 'e's invited me back there for tea
'cos Ian St John is mates with me.'

I sent off truth, and fantasy grew,
one fact left out – it was my father he knew,
a cry for acceptance, an induced fallacy,
when Ian St John waved at me.

SOFT HARRY

The story goes that a Junkers
gave birth over Soft Harry's house;
opened a broad belly above Anfield
and dropped its greased litter
through the roof,
the father being a Polish Munitions factory,
and it turned Harry soft.
Some say slates were sucked like a whirlpool
on to his head,
banged his infant mind upside down,
left him to run through the close streets,
coat flapping and perishing teeth.
Older, but not yet thirty,
with grey bristles and deep eyes
he would often go away for a while,
to a Home,
to a confined space.
Some days Harry was a machine gun
standing on Breck Road shooting buses;
on others, armed with just a pistol
shaped like a trembling fist,
he stalked the bowling green
blowing long raspberries
interspersed with a staccato laugh
which in it had no joy,
a cold cry from a land
that could not be reached.
Whilst we pretended,
with our invisible grenades,
something in Harry was permanently at war.
He would pick fights with unleashed dogs,

imagining them to be more demons
like those barking bombs
that came for him once.
During the school holidays
Harry was frequently taunted
by scruffy clusters of baying kids,
short-trousered medieval priests
pursuing someone who was left-handed.
It was to make Harry swear and spit,
that's why they did it,
so that they could then goad further
and yocker* back.
One day, when out with my mother,
Harry approached us on the same side,
his hair cut and scattered
by one of Bedlam's barbers.
I went behind my mother,
hoping to climb up the inside of her coat.
'Hello, Harry,' she said softly as we passed.
'Hello,' replied Harry,
and carried on his morning mission as a rifle,
his voice cutting the wire fence
and scrambling to freedom.
'He's not really mental, is he, Mum?'
'No, son, he's not well, that's all.'

*yocker: to spit

43 SHAW STREET

'You'll end up in 43 Shaw Street'
a doss-house of renown
'you'll end up in 43 Shaw Street'
wearing a pauper's crown
bogey-man 43 Shaw Street
winos flat out in town

'What d'yer think this is, 43 Shaw Street?'
room carefully unmade
'what d'yer think this is, 43 Shaw Street?'
sheets stained with lemonade
carbolic 43 Shaw Street
too drunk to be afraid

'This place looks like 43 Shaw Street'
football boots in the hall
'this place looks like 43 Shaw Street'
crayon scuffs on the wall
de-loused 43 Shaw Street
a rubber mattress stall

UNCLE BILLY

Uncle Billy, he was the one,
jumped ship in New York,
never came home
Did something on Broadway
with Irving Berlin
and sent letters home
written in the back
of shiny cars
wider than our road
Married three times,
moved to California,
news of Uncle Billy
became scarcer than
a repentant lion
after a kill
Couldn't decide who was
the bigger hero,
him, or Bill Shankly
He sent a picture
of himself and
don't-know-which-wife
cutting the cake
on a patty oh
Uncle Billy died
far from home
which is the same
as dying at home
but only further away
Married three times
instead of only once
'can't make his mind up'

He made his mind up
to leave here
Uncle Billy, he was the one

WAR WOUNDS

They hoe their short, dapper gardens,
opposite Anderson shelters
roses and hydrangeas now explode.

Did they really duck lead death
and stamp on scorpions
in the scuttling desert,
these wire men?

Behind their ordinary doors,
past which buses
float like corpses,
what do they hear?

A hoopoe pleading for silence?
Shrapnel slashing through canvas,
the pebbledash of combat?

If they now sleep,
how sound is their peace
in the rationed town?

They churn their flowing flower-beds
whilst their tears dive for cover.

LUNCH AT REECES

Dinner-dance emporium,
a thick piano for swirling round,
scarlet floor-length curtains
seemingly on stilts above Clayton Square,
waitresses in tea-room pinnies,
with boys like me at home.

My last request
before the firing squad
of the big school,
a window table
and a knickerbocker glory,
after that a cap, a blazer,
and a shifty cigarette.
All doomed heroes smoke.

FIRST TIME

On to the pitch I bounded
like a blind rabbit in a snowstorm
and stood in the wrong place.
Pity, it was nice there,
close to the touchline,
solitary,
just me and the iron turf,
stud marks set hard
like those star's footprints outside that theatre in
    Hollywood,
or was it California?
'Not 'dere, divvy. Over 'ere. In the scrum.'
Scrum? Scrum? What's a scrum?
I soon found out.
A scrum is a sort of human, thrashing, roaring
    crock-pot
where baking bodies steam, smell and threaten each
    other,
a therapy group for psychopaths.
I was quickly inducted
into the middle of this secret society,
taking my place on the front row
like Bonnie Langford at a Hell's Angels' meeting.
'Get de' ball back.'
Get the ball back?
Can't I just carry out some bridge work
on a pirhana, instead?
All I saw and felt
was the stinging slap of lashing legs,
a corporate cat o' nine tails
smeared in liniment,

lunging tentacles in a crazed, fibular semaphore
of injury and probable paralysis.
The scrum broke
and swarmed off like killer bees in search of
the last jar of honey in the world.
I stood up. On my face
the sweet uncomplaining smile of a village idiot
who's fallen off yet another wall.
I counted my ears
and then ran round in a petite circle
like a ballerina who'd been at the sherry.
No one else knew why I was doing this either.
Eventually,
somebody threw me the ball.
I caught it deftly and said, 'Thank you' –
seemed like a decent thing to do.
Ever been hit by a stagecoach of bull elephants
driven by a sumo-wrestler?
On it trampled,
every part of me prostrate
as the second row pogoed on my epiglottis
like medicine men representing their tribe
in the world stamping competition.
The game raged on,
with me a spindly pinball
pranging off huge, hooped flippers.
Somebody apparently won –
I think it was us,
but I could have sworn
some of us bashed me quite a lot.

Afterwards
in the dressing room
with my lower limbs
tie-dye dried in hard mud

the referee, who was my form master,
came in.
'Well done, Henderson. We play Newton-le-Willows
    Grammar next week. You'll be in the team.'
He beamed like a fat, jolly uncle whom I'd never met.
'Thank you, sir,' I lied,
and trudged to the bus stop
contemplating pain thresholds and mutilation.

STANDARD JOY

It began with the arrival of the box,
sometimes left late
until that same evening;
but mainly it came
a couple of days before.
I would pick out an occupant
and inhale the danger,
the twisted blue totem of a Roman Candle,
skinny sparklers dipped in slate,
a round triangle called Magic Mountain.
Out we would step into
the bike-chain-black backyard
under a frozen moon
that was having its own display,
a lunar peacock
strutting through the stars.
Bandaged in gaberdine and wool,
I plotted the ceremony,
gentle at first.
A squat, square pack like a radio battery
sowed golden seeds
to the unimpressed stones,
then the bullies –
rip-raps and bangers
doing nothing much but pounce and shout,
to be followed by a
Catherine Wheel,
a lit up Cossack dancer rotating on a one-pin leg.
And then the rest would perform,
reckless rockets
diving into the dark waters of night,

small wigwams burning raw,
tubes that turned purple and fell over.
And soon the agony of only one left,
with me hoping it was something immense,
a vivid comet,
a flaming planet.
Over it was in not very long,
a five-bob rhapsody,
a restrained celebration of foiled aspirations.
Yet what was that past event to me?
Inside, it was the colours I was cheering.

ABOVE THE DOVE OF LOVE

ABOVE THE DOVE OF LOVE

Above, the dove of love
dropped all his sap
on the juiceless earth
and flew furiously
at our high, hollow hearts

Bones did not break
in this plummet,
all that fell
were his feathers
like a fluttering crown

Afterwards, during the hermit
ceremony of death,
the sky came
and made soft
his waxed, wounded wings

Above, the dove of love
is known in
other orbits,
and even eagles
dare not approach.

ATTEMPTING ASCENSION

I want to love you as Christ loves you
with my heart scraped deep
from the buckled barnacles of self
the monotonous mound of I am
the turbulent stare of pride.
I want to love you as Christ loves you
with my face bathed free
from the spittle of splitting anger
just as Christ loves you
and we cannot even date the day He started.
The beauty of Him splendours from you
The harmony of Him descants from you
The wholeness of Him is present in you
The clarity of Him radiates from you
The sacrifice of Him seeps unguarded from you
The brittleness of Him is the compassion in you
The hope of Him is the breath for you
And I want to love you as Christ loves you.

TRIAL BY STORM

Great trees come down
yet this late flower
keeps its petals,
celebrating a miraculous strength,
a carnival of hope
swaying singularly in the urban driftwood,
wrenched members now burst dead
from that which was not substantial at all.

GANG RULES

Let's form a gang, just you and me
jelly for breakfast, cornflakes for tea
Let's do things that grown-ups can't do
put clothes on backwards, unlock the zoo

Let's form a gang, just she and he
swim like a lapwing over the sea
Let's throw healing at pains far too deep
confetti at funerals, no more sleep

Let's form a gang, just thou and me
a bucket and spade versus the scree
Let's wear snowshoes when the sun burns bright
then ask the Queen if she cries at night.

LOVE ALL

Thirty-fifteen:
my spinning mind set
to restring our lives
and jump over your net.

And if my bold backhand
should brush your tender knee,
would the line judge then rule
advantage to me?

Ignoring the umpire
my behaviour is brash,
I aim to control
with an overhead smash.

And if I should rage
bringing love to a halt,
with a volley of pride
that slams 'It's your fault.'

A venomous rally
to make your heart swerve,
please forgive me my love
I don't know how to serve.

STRUCTURAL ALTERATIONS

There should not be
this stoppage of words
for close inspection of the heart
indicates much to say.
Yet there are too many walls
not enough windows

We should produce
new plans and invent ourselves
present these models
and, where necessary, suggest amendments
(especially to me)
Still there are too many walls
not enough windows

Dusk is the worst time
with the buds drawn in against winter
holding life hard
in their slow-breathing seeds
Whilst, inside, there are
too many walls
not enough windows

If we are to learn anything
in these flowerless days
it is that
we will not find the healed hearts
of each other
If there are too many walls
not enough windows.

BURROWING

When we get to the centre of us
which may be the end
anyway, where we are complete,
there is love;
free of accusation
ignorant of bitterness
absent-minded
forgetting everything
but the nonsense of truth
with its memories of
walking in spice-smelling cities,
watching kingfishers slice the morning clouds
into wide portions of evermore blue.
Waking in snow and imagining the ruins of Europe,
scuffing through lizard-green forests
that grew into white mountains.
And even these are slight reminiscences,
the images of skin-shedding;
it is when we get to the unharmed earth in us,
there is love.

DECLARATION

And when your voice shakes with age
as all life's small intentions
enter their ripening slumbers
I will be with you

And when your lips anticipate the coming kiss
which will finally complete
the stretched hours of honing
I will be with you

And when your eyes
disperse once more
the tight clot of my hashed hopes
with your impossible love
I am and will be with you

A NIGHT'S WORK

KINGAIRLOCH

Nature is rowing again.
Three oyster catchers,
their spike-steps stiff,
screech and lunge.
In the shingle stalls
and on the granite terrace
an eyeless audience of mussels
and hunched limpets
has sucked itself to the rocks
in wait for the next tumbling tide.
The flapping pugilists
take their worry to the air;
below, eider ducks are their own water-beds,
heads deep in dipping dreams
on pillow-soft backs.
A bloated, bloodshot jellyfish,
a membrane of a mess,
sprawls beerily beside some pigtail seaweed;
put back in the loch,
there never was a beached hangover
but a crimson chandelier drifting.

FOOTBALL

Not so long ago
When footballers played football
instead of
opening discos, recording LPs, and having their hair
    tinted,
my father would take me to Anfield
His hand squeezing mine like an affectionate vice
Boyish, joyous, inarticulate excitement as we neared
    the Ground
Cold day,
scarf rubbing like a brillo pad against thin-necked skin
stopping off at the newsagent's on Anfield Road
One packet of Spangles
One tube of Trebor mints
Not so long ago
When hooliganism was classed
as dropping your sweetpaper on the floor
and when a writhing centre forward on the turf
usually meant at least a broken leg
My father would take me to Anfield
Not so long ago
I would look at the names in the match programme
And savour the syllables
Caress the vowels
and know that they would still be there for the next
    Home game
Not so long ago
when a contract dispute
was something that happened to people buying houses
When you could almost smell the brylcream
on the opposing fullback's head

Before Burgess's horrific prophecy of roaring hordes
of vandalous mutants
came true
My father would take me to Anfield
Not so long ago,
When television commentators were informative,
and did not resemble a town-crier having a nervous
    breakdown,
My father would take me to Anfield
Not so long ago,
When losing a game was only rather annoying,
    instead of
One sacked manager,
'The lads couldn't get it in the back of the net, Brian,
that's why we didn't score,'
removal of sponsorship,
and several written transfer requests

Not so long ago
Football was fun
Footballers played football
My father was alive
And he would take me to Anfield.

WORD PERFECT

If God
had a felt-tip pen
or perhaps a can of aerosol spray
What would He write
And where would He write it?

Would He be quirky,
like Michelangelo,
arousing curiosity through ornate scribble on the
    ceiling,
causing peering pilgrims to stand on the seats?

What eternal ponderings would be found up there
amidst the hanging forests of the spider's swaying
    kingdom
And would it be written in Hebrew?

'Moses was born in Egypt
But Jonah comes from Wales

Goliath was a giant flop

Man love your brother
But Cain wasn't Abel

Houses cleared, then flattened – we also provide a
    band,
phone Joshua for details.

I needed a doctor, so they send me social workers,
signed Job

Judas didn't need the money'

But then,
God's always written on ceilings

The burning bugle called creation's first light

The beetle-black sky at His Son's execution

The celestial graffiti of a star-scrambled night

God's been expressing
Himself
For ages.

CERTAIN RESOLUTIONS

Nation will bomb nation,
The Sun will kiss and yell
Whilst trying to feed the world this year
we'll give them AIDS as well

Wogan will be Wogan
Lebanon will scream
Liverpool will win the League
if not, some other team

People will spend holidays
in irksome traffic jams
Daffodils will leap with Spring
alongside new-born lambs

Pop songs will be written
but sheep won't safely graze
They're earmarked for experiments
involving microwaves

The Church will stand divided
as if in some deep trance
But, Christ still shines in glory
and gives us one more chance.

GOD GIVES YOU THIS DAY

God gives you this day
This giggling day
As the clouds hokey-cokey
And the bride shines as new
And the angels remember
The wine that was water

God gives you this day
This glowfully day
Gift-wrapped in paradise
As the church whoops and chuckles
At the priest's proclamation
That one joined to one
In Christ, equals one

God gives you this day
This sanctified day
As He Who flicked stars
Fizzed this
Dressed, blessed,
Entirely-for-you-day
God gives you this day

Lou and David's Wedding, 11 July 1987

BUT THEN AT WEDDINGS

But then at weddings there's always one
Bride
a blessed bouquet of nerves and beauty
arranged for love
and its many vivid flowerings
But then at weddings there's always one
Groom
awkwardly practising selflessness
and crossing out
the world's silly sentences about manhood
For later when they kiss
it is holy
it is God embracing himself
But then at weddings there's always one
Cheery Uncle
who only drinks twice a year
and shouldn't
now offering to try on all the ladies' hats
at once
But then at weddings there's always one
Confused Cousin
who sits in the wrong place
too embarrassed to move, too shy to stay
but he wrote the card with all his heart
it's just that his felt-tip leaked
But then at weddings there's always one
Gran in a nice frock
Auntie who likes to waltz
Younger Brother in a slick suit dying for a ciggie
But then at weddings there's always one
on his own

over in the corner by the jugs of water
no one knows how he does it
He even gets it to taste like wine
the best wine
the blest wine
But then at weddings there's always one.

Jeni and Dave's Wedding, 29 January 1989

FAMILY MATTERS

We are families in small houses
Privet hedges rise like tower blocks
We write poems in loud graffiti
We are lost on council walkways

We skateboard through padlocked precincts
Grilled shop-windows snarl like tigers
We play games in glass-strewn swing parks
We seek jobs in burning cities

We drop beer cans on grass verges
Flapping tabloids cling to branches
We crave love in chance glance discos
We leave home for something better

We are married, we are single
Whispering 'Why?' to life's loud jingle
Phone-in priests and chat-show friars
Counsel that there's nothing higher

We had parents who conceived us
Some in love and some just careless
We are held by bubbling fathers
We are yelled at just for being

We are friends with isolation
Who can sever such a binding?
Risen King of dereliction
Earthly Outcast – Heavenly Son.

COUNCIL HOSTAGE

The engine boils my back and I'm tied on tight
They've put glasses on me although I have perfect
    sight
And I get really frightened when left in the yard at
    night
I'm a mobile, municipal refuse worker's mascot

I wish I were a masthead on an ocean galleon
Carved in the image of a snorting, sea-sprayed stallion
But instead I have to wear this cheap St Christopher's
    medallion
I'm a mobile, municipal refuse worker's mascot

I'd like to introduce you to the boys on the truck
They are literary men who are down on their luck
They like doing the *Sun* crossword but they always get
    stuck
And I'm a mobile, municipal refuse worker's mascot

I'm strapped to this fender but I've known days of
    chintz
A Laura Ashley nursery with Beatrix Potter prints
But the parents got divorced, no more Bendick's
    bittermints
Now I'm a mobile, municipal, refuse worker's mascot

LOCAL MYSTERY

I'm the one who places
traffic cones on top of bus shelters
It doesn't mean anything
but it provokes letters to newspapers

It's me that's responsible
for decapitating belisha beacons
leaving their souls beating and blinking
at the panther-black night

I confess. I drop ice-cream
on the station concourse
That activity is not deliberate
merely flustered

I also remove strategic railings from public parks
this is my service to the weary

When drunk, and swaying like a flamingo on a
    skateboard,
I hurl silver helmets of beanshoots
at the whirlpool pavement

I discard shopping trolleys
upturned refugees in bushes
pleading for repatriation

I walk past you daily
I have various shapes
changeable expressions

I hang upside down from motorway bridges
composing slogans against oppression
One day I will write what I mean
it will say 'Notice me'
but I don't think anyone will.

THE GOSPEL OF ROD

Rod's gospel's not for the questioning few
Rod has a gospel to keep all in their pew
Rod's eyes-down-gospel will assimilate you
And this is the gospel of rod

Rod has a gospel that hushes debate
Rod has a gospel that prays 'Don't rile the State'
Rod's nighty-night gospel will not stay up late
And this is the gospel of rod

Rod has a gospel for laissez-faire brains
Rod has a gospel of stringed, soothing refrains
Rod's short, sharp gospel clamps its women in chains
And this is the gospel of rod

Rod has a gospel of men being men
Rod has a gospel that detests Tony Benn
Rod's cowering gospel is the size of a wren
And this is the gospel of rod

Rod has a gospel of very few qualms
Rod has a gospel that dare not sound alarms
Rod's tidy gospel is not showing Christ's palms
And that is the gospel of rod

ONLY AT EASTER

Whips circled and crudely landed
to lash life out of him,
or so it appeared.
Spikes were summoned
to close the stone vault,
and the sky growled.
Haughty robes of passing power
flapped through women wailing,
towards, unknowingly, the chasm of pride,
the parched well of no comfort.
How much those perished priests,
like us, didn't know.

Rising, he rose.
Risen, he remains.
His remains, apart from some ruby drops,
he took with him.
They became our passport out of death,
our living ascent from a
lifeless climate.
His scent of wounds,
in which we are now wrapped,
carried us out of that petrified place
into the calm city
where even the dust has been healed.

MEN ONLY

Only men go to war
strategically drop their military spoor
slapping cities 'til they're sore
only men go to war

Only men practise rape
assisted by daggers, venom and tape
treading flat God's holy grape
only men practise rape

Only men have no fear
consumer piercing of the stratosphere
hurling a cosmetic spear
only men have no fear

Only men make Christ white
interpret the Scriptures with flaying might
soon will come the vengeful night
only men make Christ white

Only men hammer tacks,
cure Heaven's purebreds by cracking their backs
Satan's hacks after the facts
only men hammer tacks.

PERFECT MATCH

I bought her an electric drill,
some rawl plugs and a work-mate,
a bag of concrete ready-mixed
and hinges for the back gate

And she would decorate the house
our week-ends were nirvanic
an ambient lunch made by me
courgettes and crab in aspic

We dressed in black, alternate days,
refrained from socialising.
On tubes I did not yield my seat
as that's so patronising

I was careful of her rhythms
and dates of ovulation
above the bed I pinned a chart
with times of menstruation

Our home we manicured with care
symmetrical and tidy
got into jazz and art nouveau
read Q, The Face and I-D

I bought her a brand new Aga
she left it when she crept out
my overwhelming goodness had
removed her need for some doubt

CANTRIL FARM ESTATE, 1971

The balconies are tiered,
wet, in more ways than one,
stacked up in this songless Dixieland
and as quiet as a nun.

Where now the gabbling groups
and promised silver trees?
And full, talking, thinking, public bars
for sharp men home from the seas?

Here in the New Canaan
there's nothing warm about
on a vicious December evening
like a firefly that's gone out.

THE ME SERENADE

Last year my hair was spiky
but this year I've slicked it back
and only hooligans and bozos
wear an anorak
Loadsamoney's now a hero
so I put some by for Crack
It takes a lot of daring being me

In designer surfing shirt
I cruise computer-graphic pubs
with my GXL outside
I've come a long way since the cubs
and I've just got a reminder
for my leisure-centre subs
oh it's busy, dizzy, tizzy, being me

If I'd been born a baby in the black Sudan
a swaddling, swamped, emaciated, also-ran
then I wouldn't have to fill in this investment plan
It costs a lot of money being me

Obsessed
possessed
nonetheless
depressed
so it's off to Top Shop with my bendy, friendy Access
charge-card diner-mism
I'm a credit to consumerism
as I spend, spend, spend, being me

I've got a bigger wardrobe
than perhaps Danny La Rue
I'm a hetero, metro man
with lots of useful things to do
like burning off the Lancs Constab
on the M.62
it's pretty, pretty dangerous being me

Fashion, like the sunset
burns and fades in a short span
like yo-yos, stubless chequebooks
and, of course, Duran Duran
but I've never known me long enough
to find out who I am

An image, or a mirage – which is me?
A mask beneath the make-up – where is me?
Time to buy new threads
Oh, very me

TWO RONNIES MAN

I want to be a Two Ronnies man
jaunty and jocular in a horse-brass pub
where the toilets are marked Stags and Does
I want to perfect the practice of harmless adultery
believing it to be so
but only with prostitutes
after all that's what prostitutes are for
they're not people
whatever that means
I evade loneliness
through back-slap bragging and bravado with the
    boys,
with the chaps
It's all part of being a Two Ronnies, Bob Monkhouse,
Jimmy Tarbuck, Jim Davidson, Benny Hill man
mentally pinching bottoms
women like it really you know
Bawdy chumminess conceals the quick march of age
    quite well
and despair only intrudes
when staring back at youth
to contemplate what I didn't achieve
whatever that means
The world was once my oyster
but I settled for fish fingers instead
I don't crave for youth, not me,
I just wish I was one
And now I'm a Two Ronnies man
casually neat and as regular as a garden sprinkler
There are thousands of us
somewhere between Basingstoke and Milton Keynes

decent types, quietly affluent
and not ready for death
whatever that means

THREE ROUNDS WITH AN AMATEUR TYRANT

Round One: From the bell he's after her. An upright bear, hopping from one pad to another. He tries a glancing head-swipe of 'You always say that.' She covers her face and staggers back. The ropes become her fragile cradle. No marks yet, but inside her a trickling haemorrhage of confusion seeps.

Round Two: She leaves her corner, a trouper. They clinch in which he sends her gum-shield flying. Her knees buckle, he backs off, satisfied. His point of view, the only point of view is heard.

Round Three: Another clash; she crumples. The towel of silent withdrawal is thrown in. This makes him seethe and pummel her more. Being the referee as well, he allows this. Afterwards, in the First Aid room, he visits her and says sorry. She cannot hear, he has beaten her deaf.

A WIFE MEDITATES ON HER BELOVED
FROM THE BATHROOM

He always leaves the toilet seat up
and sometimes he's splashed
It must have been a woman
who invented the pedestal mat
An expression of ironic protest
that is now essential furnishing
On waking, he makes the most bizarre noises
He sounds like a beached walrus belching
and blowing an off-key trumpet
whilst revving up a Harley Davidson
Why is this so?
Why are there bristles in the basin?
And the untidiness
What does one sock on top of the ottoman mean?
Do you take this hurricane to be your
lawful wedded husband?
Is this him being himself?
Do I feel disillusioned?
Do I feel resentful and used?
Could he cope if I screamed at him?
Can any man ever take failure?
Am I nagging or am I pleading
for the real him to be him
and hold the real me?
Why can't he be vulnerable yet strong
at the same time?
Precarious thing, love.

A.D.

Now you hate us again,
we are once more hook-nosed and haggling,
a golden calf
betrothed to the image of our own brilliance,
our red gem eyes
as hard as rifle butts.
Apparently it was us who displaced Lucifer
and inherited Jehovah's spoils;
this accounts for
sadism, infertility, madness and spite;
all the world's ailments
can be traced to us.
The bonding is over
and reconciliation is out of the question;
we should never have married out,
you quickly became a devious, savage husband.
At first
you worshipped our courage,
you recorded our triumphs in editorials
and respected our stoicism in books.
But now you describe our shelter
in bitter verses.
'Kidron's grasping canyons,
the valley of bones,
shards of which they've broken.'
We thought you could have loved us,
explained our personality to us;
but hate does not make us placatory,
just inflexible.
We can show you pictures

of what your hate did to us,
but some of us think even that
won't make you change your heart.

IF I SHOULD KISS YOU

If I should kiss you
as Christ now does,
would I mean it and would I dare?
Could I embrace and talk you through
the turmoil of your fading days?
Would my caress be a sullied stroke
or a hand of hope?
In all the phone numbers
you pursued, entertained, seduced and loved,
did you find the right man?
The one empty of deceit,
compassionate, celibate and complete.
Communion, for you, was always
the predictable business of bodies.
And men who choose women
are afraid to touch men who don't,
but I would now like to hold your hand
because of a man
that I'm in love with.
The one empty of deceit,
compassionate, celibate and complete.
With him there is no grave,
only laughter.

A LITTLE WORD OF
ENCOURAGEMENT

He had it coming to him, didn't he?
Know what I mean?
Mr Mental, Mad Lad, up there, saving the world.
Compassion, friendship, justice, love, peace –
no chance . . . especially nowadays.
It's a good time for me – nowadays.

I watched the whole thing
from start to finish.
My only complaint was, it didn't last long enough.
He went too quick . . . couldn't take it.
There were people crying and wailing . . . usual stuff,
usual humanitarian response.

He got talking to this fellow next to him . . . as you do
when you're being crucified . . . know what I mean?
Yak, yak, cross-talk . . . cross-
    examine . . . cross-your-heart-bra . . .
See, got you laughing, didn't I?
Got you mocking.
Eh, Peter, I can see your house from here.
It was a good joke, that one, wasn't it? One of my best.
Got you laughing.
Got you mocking.

He was talking to this fellow about forgiveness.
No chance . . .
that's like getting through to Directory Enquiries first
    time . . .
can't be done.

102

No one can be forgiven.
Believe me, I know what I'm talking about.
I'll always tell the truth.

SINGLE LOVE

You're a rose of many petals
But you're somewhat drab to kiss
Still, my heart thuds like an avalanche
Why can't you say words like this?

I'm devoted to your contours,
And your forward-bending knees
Are like pink bamboo in twilight hue
Why don't you say words like these?

In amorous hopes each evening
I embrace one-sided bliss
Yet imagine mutual murmurings
Why won't you make sounds like this?

Grand pianos, patent leather
With a Gershwin silk reprise,
Silver floor, the lure of pure l'amour
Why don't you have dreams like these?

There's a rumour love is freedom
But mine came wrapped with sellotape
Complete the coupon, with your postcode,
For just nine pounds ninety-eight.

LIFE AS A SNAPSHOT –
THOSE WERE THE DAYS

Those were the days,
drive-in garden centres,
the quick joy of microwaves,
binmen leaving rubbish in the hedge,
a new Jeffrey Archer novel.

Those were the days,
only four television channels,
turning up for a brain scan
only to discover the department
had closed two weeks ago,
car boot sales,
Jonathan Ross.

Those were the days,
short hair,
stylish clothes,
gang fights in the Arndale Centre,
family values, law and order, a return to morality,
Sunday trading, joining the Masons, Cecil Parkinson.

Those were the days,
Geldof raging louder than the Church,
at Enniskillen
Gordon Wilson being the Church,
lots of political parties but no opposition,
nine free newspapers a week
even though you didn't want them,
Silver Shadows in London sparkling past
beggars with thin dogs.

Those were the days,
coat-hanger car aerials,
a screen-test Jesus in the make-up trailer
– his little tomb of deceit –
rehearsing celluloid divinity,
the intimidating size of Sunday papers.
Those were the days.

GUILTY PARTY

They never tell you about the guilt
or the inconvenient grief
the liquid that became
drumming legs and a thrashing heart,
now evicted
(you were a temporary resident),
from my belly's basement.
They didn't instruct me
on how to mourn
as my clenched soul
flails aimlessly through the graveyard
that used to be me,
searching for a cross
or a headstone –
something to declare
that you once had been.
Life goes on
and then it doesn't.
They never tell you about the guilt.

They never tell you about the despair.
I want to be full of you,
to have my skin stretched by your tumbling
and stroke the taut wall between me and you,
so why am I wearing a hangman's hood?
They never tell you about the despair.

They never tell you about the loss.
The decision always explained as
'for the best',
This skewering of meekness.

They never tell you about the loss.
Was there ever anyone more innocent than you?
They never tell you.

BEHIND THESE SHEEPISH EYES

Sheep get caught in thickets
Sheep stay out in rain
Sheep fall off steep mountains
But shepherds feel the pain

    When I proclaim my heart to be a home
    of harmony and melodic contentment
    Your precise ear hears
    the out-of-tune clatter
    behind these sheepish eyes

Sheep get caught in thickets
Sheep stay out in rain
Sheep fall off steep mountains
But shepherds feel the pain

    When I script and stage humility
    To emphasise some minor achievement
    Your gaze follow-spots
    The stamping, squealing ego
    Behind these sheepish eyes

Sheep stray from their pasture
Sheep steal greening grain
But sheep are nowhere near
When the Shepherd takes the blame

    When I camouflage this holy fleece
    in sleek shades of pack approval
    You find the fragile,
    fearful infant dressing-up
    behind these sheepish eyes

Sheep stray from their pasture
Sheep steal greening grain
But sheep are nowhere near
When the Shepherd takes the blame

Some sheep even jeer
When the Shepherd takes the blame

ANOTHER NIGHT IN IRELAND

When they came it was evening,
and behind the bronze bubble-glass door
the kitchen grill was Majorca;
anaemic chips lay on their aluminium beach;
above, their sky was full of fire and blue.
Nice place, Majorca
Lots of beer
Lots of chips
No murals, no painted pavements,
nothing to point us out,
even our accents we held in
We hoped to manage it again this year

When they came it was evening.
On television Tom had crashed into Butch;
behind the kennel Jerry was giggling,
a sweet chuckle of conspiracy
a snigger of war.
Tom had walked straight into it
as Butch growled like a demon.
On the floor the children sat like owl chicks –
still, wide eyes.
What's comical about demons?

When they came it was evening.
There was a ring at the door
and he walked up the hall,
he even turned on the light for them.
The neighbours said that after the shots
there was a lot of screaming;
funny, I don't remember that at all.
The door's been fixed though.

A CONSCRIPT PROTESTS

The streets have been perfumed with tarmac
and I am wearing borrowed bones
on this moody morning
Planets have rolled across the plain of the night
churning up the clotted clouds
the sky is now the colour of slush
and celestial tank tracks scar the frail gleam of day
The stars are refugees
huddled somewhere beyond the eye,
too innumerable to name,
their life's light hiding in a loft,
fearing the tramp of troops
All around is the brooding bile of war
as God enfolds the universe
and sighs
Away from the screeching song of shells
are those with brittle empires
these perfectly trimmed holy men
these saccharine sages
these totem-pole theologians
these silvered, shining skeletons,
they are giving us what we want
And when fraught and frantic messengers
cry through their courts
announcing the dead
they are not whipped
they're just not asked back.

We are not being prepared for battle
we are not ready
we have not been warned.

FIGHTING TALK

Let us not be allies with revenge
or conspiring friends with fury
Burning tyres and nail bombs
can only be obtained from
the angry arsenal called darkness
All borrowers from this Hades for beginners
eventually develop disfigured souls,
their bowels and bladders
bubbling and boiling with bitterness
A walking-frame or a wheelchair
cannot assist a spewing spirit
Keep away from all clicking weapons
that chant a chorus for justice
but where the tune bangs out retaliation
Even though you were beaten in Babylon
bolted up in Belsen
scorched in Soweto
buried in Belfast
Make sure your sword is clean
Your armour polished pure for heaven
Retribution was never an item in your
kit inventory
The pursuit of restoration
The practice of reconciliation
that finally punctured
Jesus' lolling head,
these are your battle orders.

BEING SHAVED

I want to see the chairs that Christ carved
And sit on a stool that He shaped
When sawing and sharpening slain cedars of Lebanon
or bending olive trees into tables
Did He imagine the coming
brutal bite of beam
upon His back
The ragged pole to which He would be pinned
Glued tight against that wooden woe
Malleted in place?
He then slid off
and cut down Satan's stake
And, as for me,
Terrified at all my tawdry piety
The Holy Carpenter
now planes down my imperfections
with chipped and spliced fingers,
He bleaches the blemish of my grey grain
And chisels out
the sour knots that
protrude and poison . . .

This pure and practised Craftsman

FOR JOHN
THIS DAY IN PARADISE

This day in Paradise
new feet are treading through
high halls of gold

This day in Paradise
new legs are striding over jewelled fields in which
the diamond
is considered ordinary

This day in Paradise
new eyes have glimpsed the deep fire ready
to flame the stale earth pure

This day in Paradise
new blood, the rose-red juice that gushed at Golgotha,
now ripples and races down the pure veins
of a recently arrived beloved

This day in Paradise
a new heart pounds in praise
a new body, shaped by sacrifice

This day in Paradise
the daunting dart of death
has no point,
no place
and no meaning

And whilst we mourn and weep
through these human hours
This day in Paradise
the blazing embrace
between Saviour and son, goes on, and on, and on . . .

F. M. D.

When I was a girl
cantering past sixteen
all was so bright,
even the mosquito evenings
had the lucid, luminous moon.

Later, as a young mother
tugging some of my babies
past the wolf's breath of war,
above Blackheath, I found
it was only a short eclipse.

Then, through the giddy spring
of no more bombs
we learned new phrases,
'You've never had it so good,'
and discarded old ones,
'Put that light out.'

After all this
came the merry glow of ballgowns
skating like nimble beacons
around the candle, candelabra rooms,
and all was so bright.

In the stone bunting City of David
by the almond blossom tree
I learned the mysteries of
suffering and the necessary training
for my new address.

Now, at the end,
bright is a small, weak word
to describe the dazzling table
at which I now feast,
the candescent palace that I inhabit
with His paschal perfume smeared on the door.
But, so that you understand,
I will say once more:
Now, at the end,
all is so bright.

POEM FOR AN IRISH WOLFHOUND

Glorious in her greyness
her curious nose snorting down warrens
through heather
rabbits planning mass evacuation.
Eyes like forest fires
showing her joy to us
her excited tongue
like a manic marionette
is unpredictable.
Her jaw is the stage
her teeth the footlights
as this delicate pink puppet dances and swishes
through its exhausting performance.
Her figure the finest carving
her tail smiles at her exploits
her ears starched by concentration
hang rigid like picture hooks.
She sees a small animal . . . a rabbit perhaps;
her eyes, like brown arrows, take aim
The chase is on . . .
She explodes through the lace-like grass
with dignified contempt
If she were an aeroplane
she would be flying extremely low.
Using her tail as a rudder
she changes direction
her body leaps with grace
her legs shudder with rhythm
The chase is over . . .
The small animal has parachuted down
a prayed-for hole

She returns
head hanging between her shoulders
tongue swaying unsteadily
like an elderly duchess on an elephant.
She leans like an excited toddler
and cherishes our hugs.
Glorious in her greyness
our Ruth of Delorne.

THE LONG GIRAFFE

The long giraffe
emits no laugh
when forced to take
an evening bath
His legs don't fold
his ears get cold
his dusty frame
of patchwork gold
can only guess
the happiness
of being clean
from jungly mess

And ones that creep
and some that cheep
can float, then pierce
the silver deep
And those that roar
plus beasts that gore
can feel the wet
seep through each pore.
Whilst those with fins
enjoy gloss skins
giraffe is moist
below his shins

But I propose
that nothing glows
quite like his beam
ing gleaming toes.

PARTY NIGHT IN THE JUNGLE

It was party night in the jungle
The hunters were asleep
An elephant crept into camp
And siphoned off their jeep

Elsewhere, beyond the clearing
In a mansion no one sees
The ballroom had been polished
By a hive of busy bees

A panda poured the cocktails
Made from liquid bamboo shoots
An alligator had to leave
For wearing pink flesh boots

A spider and his mate waltzed round
Quick-stepped and did the Frug
A bat in contact lenses
Kissed a rather ugly bug

The entrance of the awesome lion
Really caused a stir
He munched a veggie burger
And flashed peace signs everywhere

A chic, high-heeled giraffe appeared
Her heart set on romance
A talcum-powdered skunk slinked off
Without being asked to dance

121

Some rhinos got quite boisterous
And fought amongst themselves
Meanwhile a peckish woodworm
Went and ate the kitchen shelves

The wild pig drank some home-brew schnapps,
Began to feel quite whoozy
A hippo squeezed himself upstairs
And climbed in the jacuzzi

A shifty looking magpie
Stole a plate of vol-au-vents
An ape crushed numerous vertebrae
Through hugging everyone

Hyenas rolled up giggling
The bouncers smelt their breath
A lisping, chinless snake remarked
'They look a fwighful meth.'

A rather well-read owl made known
His cultural pretensions
A beaver sent a sloth to sleep
Discussing home extensions

It was early in the jungle
As an ambling baboon
Shuffled past the dozing hunters
In his hand a pink balloon

It was morning in the jungle
And the sickening click of rifle
Claimed another needless tiger
By its side a bowl of trifle.

ELECTION SPECIAL

Outside the sun skids over manicured lawns
A lethargic technician gets the afternoon yawns
As a room full of creatures wonder why they were born
Such are the thoughts of a laboratory dog

In the cage next to mine there's a chain-smoking rat
Whilst down on the ground floor a steroid-fed cat
A tortoiseshell Buddha, gets hopelessly fat
The end comes so slow for a laboratory dog

Up above lolls a rabbit in urine-soaked hay
Who listens to sonar waves most of the day
He only stops jerking when the wires go away
The gaga companion of a laboratory dog

I tunnelled out once, but I didn't get far,
And before I was thrown in the back of a car
I saw other research blocks, floodlit and barred,
But they are for different laboratory dogs

On the valium walkways and wind-wailing heights
Experiments labelled 'political rights'
Are syringed into those who are too stunned to fight
A civilised maiming
persuasive defaming
a sure way of taming
a laboratory dog

AND THEY CRIED FOR JUSTICE

And they cried for justice
And justice said
'Don't eat when you're hungry
sleep in tin-foil
and enjoy loud dreams that cut and crackle,
warm your pillow in the microwave
– everyone's got one.
But whatever you do, don't get old,
you lose marks for that.'

And they cried for justice
And justice said
'You, fumbling, confused person with the white stick
listening for juggernauts and treading in dog
    excrement
Give your pale crutch to the man with no legs,
for this is our extremely flexible
Community Care Programme in action.'

And they cried for justice
and justice said
'Fear not, fee-earning citizens,
God has sent us in the nick of time
for we are acquainted with his entrepreneurial ways'

For when justice is surgically slashed,
having gone private,
asunder
All that's left is just ice,

Cold blocks of council-chamber cruelty
just ice
Callous clauses drafted by committees with charts and
    graphs
just ice
helicopters growling as masked horses
silence the shouting streets
just ice
long-lens beatings that make us shiver
just ice
blacks huddled on guttural gallows
no justice – just ice

How to melt this foul freezing?
Only blood can do it
mixing once more with water
Christ's hacked heart leaking in perpetual transfusion
brings furious and final justice
into this
just ice world

HIP-OP RAPPITY RAP

I'm sitting here on the 14th floor
in the limb replacement corridor
my X-ray of some months before
confirms just why this leg's so sore,
and I've begged the femur specialist
to eradicate my starboard list
'Please operate, make this ache desist'
he said, 'Take these pills, join the waiting list'

he put me down
he put me down
he put me down
he put me down
for a

Hip-op rappity rap
I can't stand straight, I'm a lop-sided chap
Hip-op rappity squeaks
My career is over as a kangaroo
Hip op rappity squeaks
It's not much fun when your pelvis creaks
Hip-op rappity ouch
only three more years of pain to go
and again

Hip-op rappity rap

    They'd have to treat me quick if I had something
      mean
    Like Egyptian typhoid or a ruptured spleen
    But all I've got is a permanent lean

I make Long John Silver look like Torvill and
    Dean
They said 'If you go private there's a room for you
with colour television and a tree-top view
or why not do it yourself at B & Q
with a saw and a ratchet and some super glue?'

I couldn't pay
I couldn't pay
I couldn't pay
I couldn't pay
for a

Hip-op rappity rap

Also available in Hodder Christian Paperback

UP TO DATE

Steve Turner

Bright as a light, sharp as a razor, here are poems for people who feel poetry has fogotten them. Popular and much-quoted favourites include 'Tonight We Will Fake Love' and 'Nice and Nasty'.

'At last, a poet who captures today with all the flair of a rock number.'

Peter Lewis, *Daily Mail*

'Undercuts the complacencies of right and left wing assumptions alike ... He sees the skull beneath the comfortable skin.'

D. M. Thomas, *Times Literary Supplement*

CAN YOU HEAR THE HEARTBEAT?

Dave Andrews

When Dave Andrews and his friends gave away $1,000 in $2 bills to passing shoppers, they had a riot on their hands. Dave's aim was to draw people's attention to the greed and materialism being encouraged in local elections in his native Queensland, Australia.

In *Can You Hear the Heartbeat?* Dave Andrews describes the radical alternative to a me-first lifestyle in which the strong get power and the weak go to the wall. It is a lifestyle he and his wife Ange have adopted that puts into practice God's heartbeat of love for the forgotten, broken people in the community. It is a lifestyle most people say is impossible – and crazy – to follow. It is a lifestyle based on the radical example of Jesus.

'It could be one of the ten most important books on a Christian imprint in the 1980s.'
Martin Wroe, journalist and author

'Not a book that comfortable Christians will enjoy, but one they should read.'
Dr David Penman, Archbishop of Melbourne

For twelve years Dave Andrews worked among destitute expatriate travellers in India. Now he is state representative for Tear Fund in Queensland, Australia, and is active in local community work. He is a leading speaker at Greenbelt 1989.

TRUTH AND SOCIAL REFORM

Vishal Mangalwadi

Truth and Social Reform is a remarkable and prophetic Christian message. Rooted in the author's experience of India's crippling poverty, it has wider application for Christians concerned about justice of all kinds, offering theological and economic principles in a lively and stimulating way, and issuing an agenda of thought and action to Christians in the West.

'With his credentials, and with his personality, Mangalwadi could have taken up work in academics, administration, or other fields. He chose, instead, to go back to his ancestral village to work for the upliftment of his people. He has been arrested, he has been beaten, his life has been threatened by different groups, because of his devotion to the Lord Jesus and his desire to work for the good of his people. He has been compared with Gandhi. But "a new Gandhi" is a label with which he feels extremely uncomfortable. What matters is that he has the ability to lead, to inspire, to sacrifice and to fight on behalf of the poor and the oppressed. He also actually believes in a God who can move mountains. This sort of spirituality – genuinely spiritual, powerful, and totally dedicated to the service of the poor – this sort of spirituality, I salute.'

Writer and broadcaster Prabhu Guptara from
Indian Spirituality (Grove Books)

A Spire Paperback